THE CAR

Chris Oxlade

Heinemann Library

Chicago, Illinois

www.heinemannraintree.com
Visit our website to find out more information about Heinemann-Raintree books.

To order:
☎ Phone 888-454-2279
🖳 Visit www.heinemannraintree.com to browse our catalog and order online.

© 2011 Heinemann Library
an imprint of Capstone Global Library, LLC
Chicago, Illinois

Edited by Louise Galpine and Laura Knowles
Designed by Philippa Jenkins
Original illustrations © Capstone Global Library Ltd 2011
Illustrated by KJA-artists.com
Picture research by Mica Brancic

Originated by Capstone Global Library Ltd
Printed and bound in China by CTPS

15 14 13 12 11
10 9 8 7 6 5 4 3 2 1

Library of Congress Cataloging-in-Publication Data
Oxlade, Chris.
   The car / Chris Oxlade.
      p. cm. -- (Tales of invention)
   Includes bibliographical references and index.
   ISBN 978-1-4329-3827-7 (hc) -- ISBN 978-1-4329-3834-5 (pb) 1. Automobiles--History--Juvenile literature. I. Oxlade, Chris. II. Title.
   TL147.O93725 2011
   629.222--dc22
                          2009049144

Acknowledgments
The author and publisher are grateful to the following for permission to reproduce copyright material: Alamy pp. **6** (© The Print Collector/Art Media), **22** (© Tim Woodcock); Corbis pp. **5** (© The Art Archive/Alfredo Dagli Orti), **10** (© Hulton-Deutsch Collection), **13** (© Hulton-Deutsch Collection), **19** (Bettmann/© Underwood & Underwood), **20** (© Bettmann), **25** (Reuters/© Stefan Wermuth), **27** (© Bob Daemmrich); Getty Images pp. **4** (PhotoDisc/© James Quigley), **8** (Science & Society Picture Library), **12** (Hulton Archive/MPI), **17** (Science & Society Picture Library), **23** (Time Life Pictures/Joseph Scherschel); Photolibrary pp. **11** (Imagestate/National Motor Museum), **15** (Imagestate/The Print Collector), **16** (imagebroker.net/ROM ROM), **18** (Imagestate/National Motor Museum), **21** (Imagestate/The Print Collector/Ford/Ann Ronan Picture Library); Shutterstock p. **24** (© Mark Smith); Trevithick Society p. **7** (Pete Joseph).

Cover photographs of a 2009 Tesla Roadster reproduced with permission of Photolibrary/Drive Images/Evox Productions and vintage cars in the London to Brighton Run reproduced with permission of Mary Evans Picture Library.

We would like to thank Ian Graham for his invaluable help in the preparation of this book.

CONTENTS

Look for these boxes

Biographies

These boxes tell you about the life of inventors, the dates when they lived, and their important discoveries.

Setbacks

Here we tell you about the experiments that didn't work, the failures, and the accidents.

EUREKA!

These boxes tell you about important events and discoveries, and what inspired them.

Any words appearing in the text in bold, **like this**, are explained in the glossary.

TIMELINE

2010—The timeline shows you when important discoveries and inventions were made.

THE WHEEL

People have been using wheels for thousands of years, but the first cars were made less than 150 years ago. The motorcar—also known as the automobile—is one of the world's favorite inventions. Today, there are an estimated 600 million cars in the world, and another 50 million new cars are made every year.

Car parts

A car moves along on wheels that are turned by an engine. Fuel is stored in a tank and passes into the engine, where it burns to make the engine's parts turn. An **exhaust system** carries waste gases away from the engine, and a cooling system stops the engine from getting too hot. The car has a strong, metal body that all the other parts are attached to. Gears are used for starting, driving at different speeds, and reversing. A springy **suspension** supports the body and keeps the tires touching the road. A steering wheel turns the front wheels from side to side to steer the car.

When you travel in a car, do you ever think about the different inventions that make it work?

around 3500 BCE
—Wheeled carts are used for transportation

around 2000 BCE
—Wheels with spokes begin to appear

3000 BCE   2000 BCE   1000 BCE

Without the wheel, there would be no cars. We do not know who invented the wheel or exactly when it was invented. Thousands of years ago people moved heavy things with rollers made from tree trunks. They probably made the first wheels from solid planks joined edge to edge and cut into a disc. The earliest evidence we have of wheels comes from pictures of a cart carved in pottery in about 3500 BCE (that is 5,500 years ago).

This clay model of a cart has moveable wheels. It was made in Europe during the Bronze Age (around 2300 BCE–700 BCE).

1712 CE—
Thomas Newcomen builds the first steam engine

1769—
Nicholas-Joseph Cugnot builds the first steam-powered carriage

0

1000 CE

THE FIRST STEAM CARS

In 1769 French military engineer Nicolas-Joseph Cugnot built a bulky steam-powered carriage for pulling heavy guns. Other experimental steam cars followed. Although steam engines powered some trucks, tractors, and buses, steam cars were never successful.

How a steam engine works

The parts of a simple steam engine are a boiler, a fire box, and a **cylinder** and **piston**. A fire in the fire box heats water in the boiler, producing steam. The steam travels along a pipe to a cylinder, where it pushes a piston in and out of the cylinder. In a steam car, the moving piston turns the car's wheels.

Cugnot's steam wagon was the first vehicle powered by an engine rather than an animal.

1801—Richard Trevithick tests his *Puffing Devil* steam carriage

Richard Trevithick (1771–1833)

English mining engineer Richard Trevithick began experimenting with steam engines to pump water out of tin mines. He went on to build steam engines with high-pressure boilers. These were smaller and more powerful than other steam engines. In 1801 Trevithick built a vehicle with one of his steam engines on board to move it. He called it the *Puffing Devil*. Trevithick went on to build the first-ever steam locomotive.

This working copy of the *Puffing Devil* was built 200 years after Trevithick's original.

Setbacks

Cugnot's machine was extremely slow. It needed more wood put on its fire every few minutes and eventually crashed because it had no brakes. Richard Trevithick's *Puffing Devil* was destroyed by fire. Other steam cars were heavy, inefficient, and very expensive to run.

A NEW ENGINE

In the 1850s, engineers developed a new type of engine—the **internal combustion engine**. This engine was smaller and lighter than a steam engine of the same power. It was the invention that made the first real cars possible.

Frenchman Étienne Lenoir built the first internal combustion engine in 1859. It burned gas in its **cylinder**. Lenoir's engines were not very powerful and wasted lots of gas. Most were used to operate factory machinery.

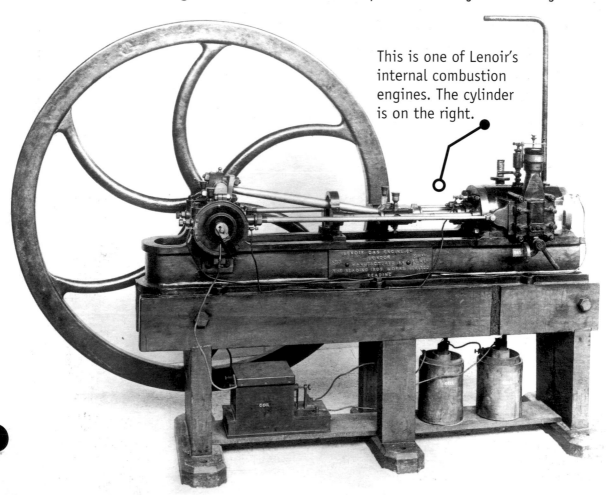

This is one of Lenoir's internal combustion engines. The cylinder is on the right.

How an internal combustion engine works

In an internal combustion engine, the fuel (which is gas or liquid) is mixed with air and burns inside a can-shaped space called a cylinder. The fuel explodes, and this explosion forces a **piston** down the cylinder. The movement of the piston turns a shaft. The piston moves back into the cylinder, and the process is repeated. In a car, the shaft turns the wheels, which makes the car move along.

EUREKA!

In 1876 German engineer Nikolaus Otto built a new type of internal combustion engine. It was a **four-stroke engine**. This meant its piston went through a series of four strokes (movements) again and again. The engine was much more efficient than Étienne Lenoir's engines. Today, this movement is known as the four-stroke cycle or Otto cycle. Nearly all modern car engines use Otto's four-stroke cycle.

fuel and air

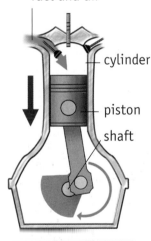

cylinder

piston

shaft

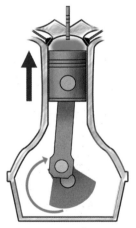

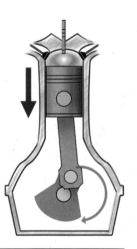

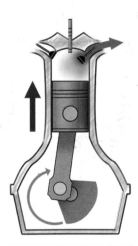

stroke 1	stroke 2	stroke 3	stroke 4
INTAKE: piston moves down, sucks in mix of air and fuel	COMPRESSION: piston moves up, squeezing fuel and air	POWER: fuel burns, pushing piston down	EXHAUST: piston moves up, pushing waste gases out

9

BETTER ENGINES

In the 1880s, two Germans named Gottlieb Daimler and Karl Benz built small, lightweight **internal combustion engines**. Both used gasoline as fuel. Despite living just 100 kilometers (60 miles) from each other, neither man knew about the other's work.

Daimler and his friend Wilhelm Maybach also invented a device called a **carburetor**. This was needed to mix the liquid gasoline with air before it went into the engine's **cylinders**. The carburetor turned the liquid gasoline into a mist of fine droplets that were carried along in the air. When the driver opened the engine's throttle, the carburetor let more air, and so more gasoline, into the cylinders. This made the engine turn faster. The carburetor was used in most cars until the 1980s.

This photograph shows Maybach (front left) with Daimler's son (front right) in an 1886 Daimler car.

Gottlieb Daimler (1834–1900)

Gottlieb Daimler started making engines when he worked at Nikolaus Otto's factory. In 1882 Daimler and his friend Wilhelm Maybach left Otto's company and went on to build their first lightweight **gasoline engine**. Daimler built his first car in 1886.

EUREKA!

The **diesel engine** was developed in 1892 by German engineer Rudolf Diesel. In a gasoline engine, the fuel is ignited by a spark plug that makes a spark using electricity. In a diesel engine, the diesel fuel ignites because it gets very hot when it is squeezed into the top of the cylinder.

11

1859—Étienne Lenoir builds the first internal combustion engine 1859—The lead-acid battery is used in most electric cars

HORSELESS CARRIAGES

The first cars were made by putting engines onto horse-drawn carriages. These "horseless carriages" were open on top and had large wheels with spokes. Most experts agree that the first real car was built in Germany by Karl Benz in 1885. Benz built a three-wheeled carriage powered by his own **gasoline engine**. Pulleys and chains from the engine turned the wheels. The car's top speed was 13 kilometers per hour (8 miles per hour).

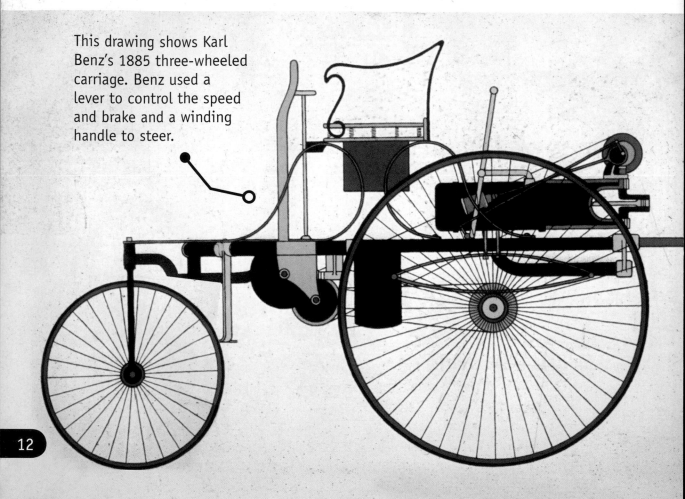

This drawing shows Karl Benz's 1885 three-wheeled carriage. Benz used a lever to control the speed and brake and a winding handle to steer.

1860—Étienne Lenoir builds a simple car

1870s—Metal wheels are developed

Karl Benz (1844–1929)

To build his first car, German engineer Karl Benz had to invent his own engine, gears, **clutch**, and **radiator**. Benz began manufacturing cars, but sales were very slow. In 1888 Benz's wife, Bertha, took a Benz car on a publicity trip with their two sons. They covered about 190 kilometers (120 miles), stopping to buy gasoline and to fix mechanical problems themselves. By 1900 Benz had sold 2,000 cars.

Setbacks

When the first cars appeared, the pedestrians, horse riders, and horse-drawn carriage drivers who already used the roads were worried. Some thought that car engines were noisy, might explode, and would frighten horses. Traveling by car was not easy. Most roads were bumpy dirt tracks. There were no gas stations or car mechanics. Drivers had to repair their own flat tires. In bad weather, drivers and passengers had to wear coats, hats, and gloves.

1876—Nikolaus Otto builds the first **four-stroke engine**

1880

THE MODERN CAR

In the late 1880s, dozens of mechanics and engineers began designing and building their own cars. Cars were built with engines at the front, at the back, and in the middle, and designers tried different ways to get power to the wheels. In France in 1891, René Panhard and Émile Levassor built a car with a layout of parts similar to that of a modern car. This layout became known as Système Panhard. The layout was popular for nearly 100 years. It had:

- a front engine

- a transmission that allowed the car to start, move at slow and fast speeds, and reverse

- a shaft connecting the transmission to the wheels driven by the engine

- a **clutch** used to disconnect the engine from the transmission (for stopping and changing gear).

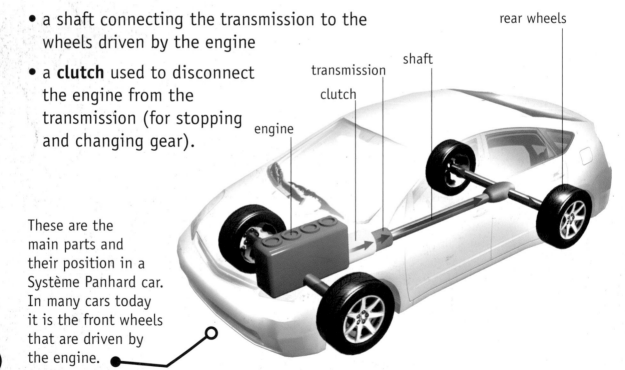

rear wheels

shaft

transmission

clutch

engine

These are the main parts and their position in a Système Panhard car. In many cars today it is the front wheels that are driven by the engine.

1883—Karl Benz forms the Benz & Cie company to make engines

1885—Benz and Gottlieb Daimler both build their first **gasoline engine**

1885—Benz builds the first real motorcar

1888—Bertha Benz takes a Benz car on a publicity drive

1888—John Dunlop invents the pneumatic (air-filled) tire

EUREKA!

In the late 1890s, a car seller in France named Emil Jellinek told Gottlieb Daimler that a fast, lightweight car would be popular. So Daimler designed one. It was unveiled in 1901 and was named the Mercedes, after Jellinek's daughter. The Mercedes had lots of new and improved features. The **chassis** and frame were made of steel instead of iron and wood, and the body was low and **streamlined**. It had a powerful four-**cylinder** engine and a honeycomb **radiator**. The Mercedes was a big success in many car races.

This is the first Mercedes car, built in 1901.

Innovations

There have been hundreds of innovations during the history of the car. They have made cars easier to drive, more comfortable, more reliable, faster, and more efficient. Here are just a few:

Pneumatic tires (1845)
Robert William Thomson invented pneumatic (air-filled) tires, but John Dunlop, a Scottish vet, manufactured them first. He made them for bicycles. It was French engineer André Michelin who first tried putting them on cars.

Automatic gears (1937)
Fully automatic gears were invented and first appeared in Buick and Oldsmobile cars in the United States.

The air bag (1952)
The air bag was invented by American John Hetrick in the 1950s, but air bags were not used in cars until the 1970s.

Anti-lock braking (1971)
An electronic anti-lock braking system (**ABS**) was developed by Chrysler and Bendix.

The Citroën Avant of 1934 was the first widely successful car to have front-wheel drive.

1901 —The first Mercedes is completed

1903—Henry Ford starts the Ford Motor Company

1908—Ford makes and sells the first Model T car

In 1933 Englishman Percy Shaw noticed that cat's eyes reflect light very well. This gave him the idea for inventing reflecting studs to mark lines in roads. The studs can now be seen at night on roads all over the world.

André Citroën
(1878–1935)

After World War I (1914–18), Frenchman André Citroën converted his ammunitions factory into a car factory. His most famous car was the Citroën Traction Avant of 1934. This was the first car with a metal shell called a **monocoque** (or unibody), which made it very tough. The company dropped one down a cliff to show just how strong it was. Despite the company's success, Citroën lost all his money through gambling.

1913—Ford Motor Company begins using a moving **assembly line**

1914—Ford makes 200,000 Model Ts in a year

CAR MANUFACTURING

Only a few years after Karl Benz had made the first car, dozens of car-making companies had been set up in the United States and Europe. At first the cars were made individually in small workshops. But soon manufacturers turned to mass production. All the car parts were made at the same time by different workers, then put together to make the cars.

Ransom Eli Olds was one of the first manufacturers to use mass production. In 1899 he set up the Olds Motor Works in Detroit, Michigan, the city that went on to be the center of U.S. car manufacturing. By 1904 the factory had made about 5,000 Oldsmobiles.

This is the Oldsmobile Curved Dash. It was one of the first Olds cars.

1925—Ettore Bugatti builds his first Type 37 sports car

1927—Harley Earl begins working for General Motors

Henry Ford (1863–1947)

Henry Ford was born on a farm near Detroit. He did not want to become a farmer and trained as an engineer instead. In 1903 he founded the Ford Motor Company. Ford's most successful car was the Model T, which he designed to bring motoring to the masses. It was introduced in 1908 and became instantly popular. By 1913, with a moving **assembly line** churning out Model Ts, the Ford Motor Company became the world's biggest car manufacturer. In 1914 half the cars bought in the United States were Fords.

1933—Percy Shaw
 vents the reflecting
road stud

1934—Citroën
introduces the
monocoque in his
Traction Avant car

The Model T

Henry Ford's Model T is probably the greatest success story in the history of the car. It worked well for two reasons. First, Ford and his team of engineers designed the Model T to be a small car that the average American could afford to buy and run. Second, Ford manufactured the Model T on a moving **assembly line**, which made it quick and cheap to build. The first Model T was sold in 1908. When production stopped in 1927, nearly 15 million Model Ts had been assembled.

The Model T was simple and reliable. Its **chassis** was made of a new material of the time, vanadium steel alloy, that made it lightweight but strong and long lasting. It was nicknamed the "Tin Lizzie."

By 1920 one million cars a year were rolling out of Ford's factory. The cars in this photograph are finished and ready for delivery.

EUREKA!

The Model T car was so popular that Henry Ford opened a new factory at Highland Park, Michigan, in 1910. In 1913 the world's first moving assembly line began operating here. Workers added parts as the cars moved through the factory on a conveyor belt. Components, such as engines and wheels, were made on their own assembly lines so that they were ready to be installed in the cars. The moving assembly line sped up production amazingly. In 1912, before the assembly line, the Ford Motor Company made 64,000 Model Ts. In 1914 it made 200,000.

This photograph shows the moving assembly line at Ford's factory in 1913.

1952 — John Hetrick invents the air bag

1953—The first Chevrolet Corvette is introduced

1959—The Mini is introduced in the United Kingdom

1960

Italian style

Italy is home to many of the world's great car stylists. They include Ettore Bugatti and his son Jean, who designed beautiful sports cars in the 1920s and 1930s. Bugatti cars became famous for their wins on the racetrack, especially at Le Mans, France. Another famous Italian stylist, Battista Farina, known as Pinin Farina, designed cars for Ferrari, including the classic Ferrari F-40.

This 1929 Bugatti car is still being raced today.

EUREKA!

In the late 1950s there was a worldwide shortage of fuel caused by a military conflict in the Middle East, known as the Suez Crisis. Much of the fuel for cars came from that region. The British Motor Corporation asked stylist Alec Issigonis to design a small car that would not use a lot of fuel. The result was the famous Mini, which first appeared in 1959.

Harley Earl *(1893–1969)*

Harley Earl was born in Hollywood, California. His father designed and made car bodies, often for movie stars. Earl also became a car stylist. His big break came in 1927, when he was asked to design a car for General Motors. It was a success, and Earl was employed by General Motors as director of its new Art and Color Division. He stayed until 1958 and was responsible for General Motors' first sports car, the Chevrolet Corvette.

1971—Anti-lock breaking system (**ABS**) is developed

INTO THE FUTURE

Chemicals in car **emissions** pollute the **atmosphere** and are contributing to the **greenhouse effect**, which is causing **global warming**. Political problems in some oil-producing countries, together with changes in the world economy, create high fuel prices. If we want to continue to drive cars in the future, we need to invent ways to use less **fossil fuel** or to use **renewable energy** instead.

Power stations that burn fossil fuels give out gases that pollute the atmosphere.

1990—General Motors shows a **prototype** electric car, the Impact

Electric cars

An electric car is a car that has an electric motor instead of a **gasoline** or **diesel engine**. The motor gets electricity from rechargeable batteries and turns the car's wheels. The batteries are recharged by plugging a cable from the car into an electrical socket. Electric cars are "zero-emission" vehicles and are also very quiet. However, the electricity they use is normally made in power stations that are powered by fossil fuels, so electric cars are not totally "green."

The first electric vehicle was built way back in the 1830s. By 1900 electric cars were very popular. Around 25 percent of all the cars in the United States were electric, including many New York taxis.

Setbacks

Electric cars sound amazing. But they have one major problem. The batteries needed to work an electric car's motor run out of electricity quite quickly, so the car has a limited range. Modern electric cars can travel about 160 kilometers (100 miles), but take hours to recharge.

This electric car is plugged into a charging station on a street in London, England.

1997—Toyota introduces the Prius, the first modern hybrid car

2000

Hybrid cars

A hybrid car has both a **gasoline engine** and an electric motor. In some hybrid cars the gasoline engine and the motor drive the wheels around. The motor gives a boost when the driver wants to accelerate quickly. In other hybrid cars the gasoline engine turns an electricity generator that provides power for the electric motor. Hybrids use much less fuel than normal cars. The first modern hybrid car was the Toyota Prius of 1997, but the idea is not new. The first hybrid car appeared in 1900.

Hybrid and electric cars normally have "regenerative" braking. When the car slows down the motor works as a generator, making electricity that recharges the batteries.

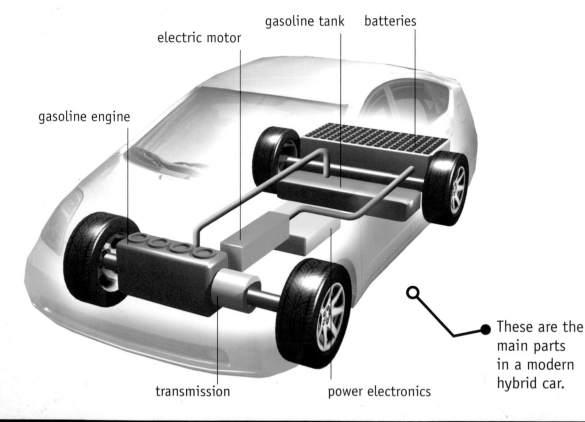

electric motor

gasoline tank   batteries

gasoline engine

transmission

power electronics

These are the main parts in a modern hybrid car.

2008—The Solar Taxi experiment car drives around the world

Current developments

Cutting-edge car technologies include fuel-cell electric cars and solar cars. Fuel cells use hydrogen gas to produce electricity and give off only water. Solar cars use energy from the sun to make electricity to power their motors.

Solving problems

Modern cars are very complicated machines. They are crammed full of electronics and other systems that keep the engine running properly, give information to the driver, and keep the passengers safe. Even so, many more innovations are needed if we want to continue using cars in the future, without adding to the environmental problems they have already created.

These experimental solar-powered cars are taking part in a solar car race across North America.

TIMELINE

around 3500 BCE
Wheeled carts are being used for transportation

around 2000 BCE
Wheels with spokes begin to appear

1712 CE
Thomas Newcomen builds the first steam engine

1885
Benz builds the first real motorcar

1885
Benz builds his first **gasoline engine**

1883
Karl Benz forms the Benz & Cie company to make engines

1876
Nikolaus Otto builds the first **four-stroke engine**

1885
Gottlieb Daimler builds his first gasoline engine

1886
Daimler builds his first car

1888
Bertha Benz takes a Benz car on a publicity drive

1908
Ford makes and sells the first Model T

1903
Henry Ford starts the Ford Motor Company

1901
The first Mercedes is completed

1900
Porsche builds the first hybrid car

1913
The Ford Motor Company begins using a moving **assembly line**

1914
Ford makes 200,000 Model Ts in a year

1925
Ettore Bugatti builds his first Type 37 sports car

2008
The Solar Taxi experimental car drives around the world

1997
Toyota introduces the Prius, the first modern hybrid car

1990
General Motors shows a **prototype** electric car, the Impact

1769
Nicholas-Joseph Cugnot builds the first steam-powered carriage

1801
Richard Trevitick tests his *Puffing Devil* steam carriage

around 1830
The first electric car is bult

1870
Metal wheels are developed

1860
Lenoir builds a simple car

1859
The lead-acid battery, used in most electric cars, is invented

1859
Étienne Lenoir builds the first **internal combustion engine**

1888
John Dunlop invents the pneumatic (air-filled) tire

1891
René Panhard and Émile Levassor design the Système Panhard

1892
Rudolf Diesel invents the **diesel engine**

1899
Ransom Olds opens his Detroit factory

1897
The Stanley twins build their first steam car

1896
Henry Ford builds his first motorcar

1927
Harley Earl begins working for General Motors

1933
Percy Shaw invents the reflecting road stud

1934
Citroën introduces the **monocoque** in his Traction Avant car

1971
An anti-lock breaking system (**ABS**) is developed

1959
The Mini is introduced in the United Kingdom

1953
The first Chevrolet Corvette is introduced

1952
John Hetrick invents the air bag

GLOSSARY

ABS stands for **a**nti-lock **b**raking **s**ystem, which prevents the wheels from locking up and skidding when the driver applies the brakes

assembly line line in a factory along which a product moves as it is put together

atmosphere layer of air that surrounds Earth

carburetor device that mixes tiny drops of liquid fuel and air to be sucked into an engine's cylinders

chassis framework that supports a car's body, engine, and other parts

clutch device that disconnects a car's engine from its transmission. It is used to change gear or when the car is stopped with the engine running.

cylinder can-shaped space in which a piston slides up and down. In an internal combustion engine, fuel burns in cylinders, making the pistons move.

diesel engine internal combustion engine that uses diesel oil as its fuel

emissions gases that come out of a car's exhaust system and go into the air

exhaust system system of pipes that carries waste gases away from an engine

fossil fuel fuel formed over millions of years from the remains of ancient plants and animals. Oil, gas, and coal are fossil fuels.

four-stroke engine engine in which the pistons go through a sequence of four movements each, again and again, one of which produces power

gasoline engine internal combustion engine that uses gasoline as its fuel

global warming gradual increase in the temperature of Earth's atmosphere

greenhouse effect natural effect that traps heat from the sun in Earth's atmosphere

internal combustion engine engine in which the fuel burns inside the engine's cylinders

monocoque strong shell that supports all the parts of a car

piston part of an engine that slides up and down inside cylinders. The moving piston turns the engine's shaft.

prototype first version of a car or other machine, made to test how it works

radiator part of a car's cooling system. Air flowing around the radiator cools water inside the radiator that has been heated by the engine.

renewable energy energy generated from natural resources, such as sunlight, wind, and waves, that will not run out

streamlined has a shape that allows air to flow smoothly over it as it moves along

suspension system of springs that supports the body of a car on its wheels

FIND OUT MORE

Books

Chapman, Giles. *The Illustrated Encyclopedia of Extraordinary Automobiles*. New York: Dorling Kindersley, 2009.

Graham, Ian. *How Machines Work: Fast Cars*. North Mankato, Minn.: Smart Apple Media, 2009.

Mitchell, Don. *Driven: A Photobiography of Henry Ford*. Washington, D.C.: National Geographic Society, 2010.

Websites

Find out more about Henry Ford and the Ford Motor Company at:
www.ford.com/about-ford/heritage

This website has useful information on how car engines work:
www.howstuffworks.com/engine.htm

Find out the latest news about hybrid cars at:
www.hybridcars.com

Places to visit

The Henry Ford Museum
20900 Oakwood Boulevard
Dearborn, Michigan 48124
www.thehenryford.org

Petersen Automotive Museum
6060 Wilshire Boulevard
Los Angeles, California 90036
www.petersen.org

INDEX